Blessed Easter, Brandon!
We love you so very much
dear son and we believe
great things for you.

ON THE CLOUDS TO CHINA

Affectionately yours,
Dad & Mom.
March 26, 1989

ON THE CLOUDS
TO CHINA

The Story of Hudson Taylor

by
CYRIL DAVEY

LUTTERWORTH PRESS
GUILDFORD, SURREY

First paperback edition 1974
Second impression 1982

ISBN 0 7188 2185 8

PRINTED IN GREAT BRITAIN
BY EBENEZER BAYLIS & SON, LTD,
THE TRINITY PRESS, WORCESTER, AND LONDON

CONTENTS

1

THE CHEMIST'S SHOP

"CHINA, did you say?"

"That's right, sir," answered Hudson.

The minister stared at him, sitting on a hard, straight-backed chair, and thought how frail he looked. Almost as if the wind would blow him away, he said to himself. Never been very well all through his childhood, he went on thinking, and had to give up his first job because his eyes were giving him trouble. Now, at seventeen, he marches into the house with a crazy idea and expects to be taken seriously. He shook his head slowly, as if he had not heard properly.

"You mean, you want to go to *China* as a missionary? But . . . but . . . my dear boy, you've hardly begun to grow up yet."

"I've been working for four years, sir."

"But you're just a chemist's assistant. You're not even a minister."

Hudson's eyes had a far-away look in them. "I don't want to be a minister, sir. I just want to be a missionary to the people who have never heard of Christ."

7

The minister rose to his feet, an impressive, bearded figure, and started to pace up and down the room. Every now and again he stopped in front of the young man and looked down at him, talking all the time. "You must be mad to think of it . . . China is right at the other side of the world . . . it takes six months to get there . . . there are only one or two ports where Europeans can live in safety . . . if you try and make your way into the interior you'll be mobbed and killed . . . you know what the Chinese call Europeans, don't you, boy?"

"Pink devils, sir!"

"It's not surprising the missionary societies won't send men to China. They'd just be sending them to their death. And besides, even if they wanted to they haven't enough money. Think of all the work they have to maintain in Africa, India, the South Seas and so on."

Hudson stood up, a slight, pale-faced youth not yet tall enough to stand face to face with his older friend. "Then I must pay my own way, that's all—and earn my living when I get there. I'm sorry you think I'm mad." Suddenly he grinned, and broke into a laugh. "I expect it does sound a bit daft."

Perhaps it was because the boy could still laugh at himself that the minister had a queer feeling that Hudson was not as crazy as he sounded. He crossed the room and put his arm round his shoulders. "Just give me one good reason for leaving Yorkshire and going off to the other side of the world, and I'll lend you the biggest book on China that I've got."

"That's easy," replied Hudson Taylor. "God has told me to go."

*　　*　　*

Hudson had always been a little frightened of his father. This was hardly surprising. Mr. Taylor, a chemist in Barnsley, was a strong, masterful man with a big voice. It boomed out in the shop, and even louder in the Yorkshire chapels where he preached. At home, Hudson and his brothers and sisters sat up sharply when he spoke to them. His eyes were as compelling as his voice, and there were strange stories of people whom he had cured, not by medicines from his shelves, but by sending them to sleep and telling them the pain would be gone when they wakened. There was an even queerer tale of a dog whose barking nearly drove the neighbours to distraction. Mr. Taylor hypnotised it one day and it never barked again, so they said.

Of one thing young Hudson was certain. His father was not going to hypnotise *him* into doing something that he did not want to do.

"Don't forget your great-grandparents used to entertain John Wesley."

"Always remember that your grandfather was a Wesleyan preacher."

"There's a good book here; I'd like you to read it."

Hudson sometimes wished that good books were not so common in the house—and that good people were not so dull. He would rather have worked in the bank than in his father's shop, but it was no use. As a child he always seemed to be ill with one disease or another, so that for all but two years he had never been to school at all. Instead, his mother, a gentle and kindly woman, had had to teach him all he knew. When he finished with school and started working in the bank his eyes began giving trouble and he had to come home to serve behind the counter in the chemist's shop. Sundays were sometimes very gloomy indeed.

It was on a Sunday afternoon in the summer of 1849, when his father was out preaching and his mother away from home, that Hudson looked over his father's bookshelves for something to read. Sermons, tracts, theology—dull stuff all of it. He turned away, picked up a booklet from his father's desk and strolled out into the June sunshine. In a shed he settled down on a pile of straw to read himself to sleep. The duller the book the better; the sooner he would be asleep.

But young Hudson did not go to sleep after all. As he read, it seemed as if God Himself were speaking to him in the pages of the little book. When he had finished reading he went straight indoors, knelt down by his bed and made a promise. "Lord God," he said, "for the rest of my life I will do whatever You want and go wherever You send me."

*　　*　　*

Now he worked harder than ever in the shop, and turned more frequently to his father's library. On the shelves was an atlas and Hudson could remember the day, ten years earlier, when his father had bought it. He recalled how his father had riffled through the pages, and then turned carefully to map after map. It was a missionary atlas, containing maps of all the areas in which the missionary societies were at work.

"Maps of Africa, Ceylon, India, the South Seas," his father had said. "Maps of almost everywhere—except China. Why can't the Church send workers to China? Even if it is a 'closed land' to foreigners, surely God could find a way in for them if they were sent?"

Perhaps it was because of the atlas, or because of Mr. Taylor's interest in China. Perhaps it was because—although he did not know it until years later—his father had knelt down when Hudson was born and asked that God would one day make him a missionary to China. Whatever the reason, whenever Hudson found himself day-dreaming in the shop it was always about a land of temples and mandarins, wide plains and towering mountains. Later that same year, just before Christmas, Hudson seemed to hear a voice speaking to him. The words were quite clear, though there was no one else in the room.

"I want you to go for Me to China."

It was soon after this that Hudson Taylor went to talk things over with his friend, the Congregational minister, and came home with a big book about China under his arm. The more he read the more he wanted to know. Soon he was asking another friend to get him a copy of the Bible in Chinese from the Bible Society in London. When the little parcel arrived it was not a whole Bible but only a copy of St. Luke's Gospel. As he opened it and showed it to his family they stared in astonishment at the extraordinary "letters", printed in lines which ran straight down the page instead of across it.

"What queer letters!" said his sister, Amelia.

"Oh, they're not letters at all, really," answered Hudson. "Each sign is really a separate word."

"But they're printed down the page," she went on.

"Oh yes. Didn't you know? They write downwards instead of across. And you start at the right-hand side and work backwards. You see, the back of the book is really the beginning." Hudson felt rather clever that he already knew so much. Amelia's next question left him flat.

"What does it say, Hudson? Here—on this page?"

"I don't know." Amelia giggled at his discomfiture. "I've only just got the book." Suddenly he found he was joining in the laughter against himself. "I've still got to start learning how to read it."

Hudson's enthusiasm for learning Mandarin did not last long. With no one to teach him how to pronounce the unfamiliar signs he soon had to give up, but instead he began to study Latin, as well as Greek and Hebrew in order to read the Bible in the languages in which it was written. To toughen himself he began taking long, lonely walks over the moors and dales, and so that he would be ready to sleep on the floors of Chinese inns he asked his mother to remove the fluffy feather-bed and give him a hard mattress instead.

* * *

One day his father asked a question which had been puzzling Hudson for some time. "What are you going to do when you get to China—if ever you do?"

Hudson ignored the last part. "Preach, of course."

13

"Aye, lad—you'll preach right enough. But will they listen? China's full of poverty and disease. Will they believe that God loves them, even if you tell them so? Don't forget you're a foreigner, and they're likely to think you're being paid good money for converting them!"

Hudson was silent for a moment. "I must *show* them, then. Try and heal their bodies. Perhaps that's why I was born a chemist's son." He smiled at his father as he went on. "But I shan't be able to use some of *your* methods on them . . . hypnotise them and tell them they're better. I need to know something about medicine." He went on hurriedly. "I shan't have time to become a fully-fledged doctor, of course. I *must* get to China before I'm much older."

"Eh, lad—you're only eighteen, even now. You've plenty of time to learn a bit of doctoring before the boat sails." His father's smile faded. "I wish I were sure one of the big missionary societies—our own Wesleyan one, for instance— would send you and look after you properly if you get there. You can't go on your own, lad!"

"God has told me He will send me—and He always keeps His promises."

Mr. Taylor gripped his son's shoulder for a moment. "Aye, we can't argue about that. Keep on believing it and you won't go far wrong." He rose to his feet. "But about this doctoring business.

Your mother and I have been talking it over. You know your uncle in Hull has a brother who's a doctor—Dr. Robert Hardey?"

Hudson's eyes gleamed excitedly as he guessed what was coming. "Yes," he said.

"Well, he's willing to have you to live with him for a while. He'll be able to show you enough to start you off. You'll get some salary, too. Not much, of course—but enough to pay your fare to London eventually."

"London?"

"Aye, lad. London. If you're going to be a missionary doctor in China you'll need a bit of training in a hospital first."

2

FROM DRAINSIDE TO CHEAPSIDE

THE flickering gas-lights did little more than throw pools of yellow light on to the slimy roadway, and the two men picking their way through the dirt passed from one patch of darkness into another. Now and again one of them slipped or struck his foot against a stone or a pile of garbage.

"It's a poor place to be bringin' your honour, to be sure," apologized the leader. "But then," he went on, "it's a poor place to live in, too, if it comes to that."

Hudson was too busy trying to find his way to answer the Irishman ahead of him. They moved away from the cottages bordering the canal and began to burrow through the alleyways leading into the heart of the slums. Here and there curious bystanders, almost hidden in the shadows, watched them suspiciously. "It's the Protestant preacher," he heard an Irish voice say, and remembered that when he had been here in the daytime the slum-dwellers had threatened to stone him if he came again. His guide spoke softly to the figures in the shadows. "He's on an errand of mercy." The threatening movements stopped and the watchers slunk back into the doorways.

Hudson had been in Hull for a month or two when the Irishman came to the door one evening. At first he had lived with Dr. Hardey at his own home, and then moved out to live with his aunt, but following his determination to live hard, in preparation for the day when he could go to China, he had moved once more. This time it was to a small cottage facing the canal. The folk who lived in the area never referred to it as the canal; they always called it "t' drain", flinging their rubbish, garbage and slops into it. This unsavoury area was commonly known as "Drainside". Here, with three biscuits and half a herring for breakfast, two pennyworth of prunes for dinner and some biscuits and an apple for his supper, Hudson made his home. Because of his almost starvation diet he was able to give away two shillings out of every three that he earned. A great deal of it went to the poor people he visited as Dr. Hardey's assistant, in the slums and poorer quarters of Hull. It left little enough for himself, especially as the doctor often forgot to pay him until days or weeks after the money was due.

*   *   *

When, that dark evening, his landlady called

him to see an Irish labourer outside the door Hudson was afraid the man had come to ask for money. It would have been no use if he had, thought the doctor's assistant, for he had only half a crown in the world to buy his own food and pay for his lodgings. But it was not money the man wanted after all.

"My wife is dying, sir. I want you to come and pray with her. I'm a Roman Catholic meself, but the priest won't shift from his home unless I pay him one and sixpence first. I haven't got the money, y'r honour."

If it was only to pray with her he could manage, thought Hudson, although the slum-dwellers had torn up his tracts only a few days before and driven him out. When he arrived at the room, however, Hudson was not sure that praying with the woman would be much use. She lay on a filthy mattress, with a new-born baby by her side. Half a dozen ragged children whined and whimpered with hunger. Would God take much notice of his prayer if he did not do what he could to help? he wondered. And yet there was nothing he *could* do. He *must* keep enough money to pay his way. He knelt on the dirty floor and prayed that God would heal the woman and help her.

"Can't you help us just a little bit yerself, sir?" Hudson tried not to listen to the man by his side.

"Just a shilling or so would keep her from starving and save her life." Hudson rose and went to the door. "A copper would buy her a drop of milk," the voice went on.

"I've only got half a crown." Hudson wanted to say the words and found he could not. Instead, he thrust his hand into his pocket, drew out the coin, handed it to the man and hurried out into the dark street. Strangely enough, though he now had no money at all, he felt light-hearted rather than worried. If God had sent him to see the poor woman and help her, he must trust Him for what happened next.

The following morning he was eating an apple for breakfast when his landlady came in. "'Ere's your parcel, Mister," she said, thrusting a slim brown-paper package towards him.

Hudson took it curiously and began to pull off the paper. He was not expecting anything, and could not imagine what it was. As he opened it he stared in perplexity at the pair of kid gloves it contained. There was no sender's name, no address. He started to try on one of the gloves and it fitted perfectly. Then the other—but this time his fingers stuck against something hard. A golden half-sovereign lay gleaming in his palm.

*　　*　　*

Never, to the end of his life, did Hudson Taylor

forget the half-crown and the half-sovereign. He was certain, from that moment onwards, that God would never fail those who trusted Him. If he gave what he had to God's work he would never make a fortune. There might be times when he would have nothing in the bank at all. But God was his Father, and would always provide for him. From that day forward, Hudson gave himself completely to doing God's work, leaving God Himself to provide what was needed to carry it out.

It was after another visit from the postman that Hudson began to see the future a little more clearly. He had written to a small missionary society, the China Evangelisation Society, asking if they could help him to fulfil his dream of going to China. Their reply was encouraging. They would be glad to send him, pay his passage and give him a small salary when he reached Shanghai. They suggested, however, that he should attend a year's course at the London Hospital first. Nothing could have fitted better into his own ideas.

He handed in his notice to Dr. Hardey, grateful for the way he had introduced him to the daily work of doctoring; thanked Mrs. Finch, his landlady, for her care of him; and went home to share his good news with his parents. As the coach rattled over the cobbles of the market-square outside the chemist's shop he could not foresee that, before he staggered out of the coach here the next time, he would have been given up for dead.

It was partly his old landlady Mrs. Finch's fault that he got into difficulties. Her husband was a sailor and the shipping company which employed him had an office in London. From here they sent Mrs. Finch each month some of her husband's pay. This was sensible and helpful, but they charged a good deal for doing so, and his landlady asked Hudson if he could help her by collecting the money and sending it on himself. *He* would not charge nearly as much as the shipping company for doing so. Hudson made a promise to help her readily enough, without realising the trouble he was facing.

His lodgings were in Soho, not far from Piccadilly, but a hundred years ago even the middle of London was still almost in the country. Hansom-cabs and omnibuses rattled over the rough streets, the sky above was blue and unshrouded by smoke and to walk for a mile or so was full of interest. Hudson certainly did his share of walking, too. At the hospital he was a student, earning nothing, and though he had saved a little money it was only enough to pay for the same sparse diet he had lived on at Drainside. To save money he walked to and from the hospital every day—four miles each way.

He had only been in London for a few weeks

when he heard from Mrs. Finch. The rent was almost due. Could he collect her money and send it on? The shipping office was in Cheapside, which involved a walk of another two miles. Hudson put off going to the office for a day or so, sent Mrs. Finch the money out of his own small store and, towards the end of the week, went to collect seaman Finch's pay. He was shocked at the clerk's news.

"I'm afraid there isn't any pay to collect, sir."

Hudson thought the young man had made some strange mistake. "But there *must* be some. He is a sailor on one of your ships."

"That's where you're wrong, sir. He *was* on our ship. But he deserted it in some port or other. Here it is. Look." He picked up a sheet of paper from the desk with a list of the ship's crew. "Finch. Deserted to go to the gold-fields. They had to take on another man in his place."

"But I've already sent his wife the money."

"Well, sir"—the clerk looked at him pityingly, as if he were out of his mind for doing anything so foolish—"that's hardly our concern, is it?" He put the paper down on the desk. "Good morning, sir. I'm sorry, but . . . well, there it is."

*　　　*　　　*

Perhaps Hudson was a little less careful than

usual in the days that followed, wondering how he was going to manage. Perhaps, as he sewed up some loose papers into a home-made note book, he was imagining sailor Finch digging for gold. At any rate, he stabbed his finger with the needle. Usually such a thing would have made no difference, but next day the students at the hospital had an unpleasant task to perform. The body they were dissecting was that of a patient who had died of fever, and the professor had warned them to take great care. If they had even a scratch on their hands they must not touch it. Hudson worked on with the others. Then, suddenly, he felt faint and sick. One of his friends caught him before he fell to the floor. Only when the professor coldly asked him what was the matter did he remember the needle-prick. As soon as he mentioned it the doctor shrugged his shoulders.

"That's it. That's the way the poison got into you." He looked slightly more human. "I'm sorry, young fellow, but you're finished. Go outside, get a cab and drive home as fast as you can. Say good-bye to your friends and put things in order at home. You'll be dead by the morning."

Unable to pay for a cab, Hudson scrambled on to a horse-bus. Back in Soho he was almost too weak to crawl up the stairs and it was hours later that the cousin with whom he shared his lodgings discovered him. The doctor whom the young man summoned thought it might already be too late to save his life.

"Does he drink much?"

"No beer or spirits, or anything of that sort. Only water."

"Does he smoke?"

"No. He's always lived pretty hard since he's been here."

"Good." The doctor straightened up and began to give sharp orders. "In that case we may manage to pull him through." He wrote a prescription. "Another hour or so, though, and there wouldn't have been a chance of it."

*   *   *

Hudson did get better, but it was a long, worrying illness that followed his collapse. An uncle, living nearby, moved him into his own house and saw that he was carefully nursed and given plenty of good, nourishing food. The doctor came often, astonished both by the patient's recovery and by his conviction that he was getting better simply because God still intended him to go to China. He was so deeply impressed by his faith that he refused to take any money for his attention and visits. Hudson insisted that he must at least pay for the quinine he had been given as medicine and, when at last the doctor reluctantly agreed, wondered where he would get the money. Something made him think of Finch and the shipping office and he determined to go once more in case the sailor had perhaps come back after all. Next day, though the doctor had assured him that he would not be able to walk for more than a few yards without collapsing, he slowly staggered the whole two miles to Cheapside, ending by clambering up the stairs almost on his hands and knees. As soon as he opened the door and the clerk looked up he knew he had been right.

"My dear sir, I'm *so* glad you've come." The man came forward and found him a chair. "You don't look well at all. You must have lunch with me. I owe you something more than your lunch for all the trouble you've had. You see, it wasn't your man Finch that ran away at all. Another chap of the same name. Careless of us to get them mixed up. The money is here, waiting for you— but I didn't know how to get hold of you, sir."

Hudson closed his eyes with weariness and relief and quietly thanked God for sending him back to the shipping office. Now he would have enough money to pay the doctor, go home for a while to recover and continue his studies at the hospital to the end.

It was a few days later that he walked round to the headquarters of the China Evangelisation Society and was ushered into the office of the secretary, Mr. Bird. "I haven't written to you for some time," Hudson introduced himself. "I thought I should come and see if you still wanted me."

Mr. Bird smiled as he picked up a letter from his desk. The ink was still not dry where he had signed his name. "But I've just written to you, Mr. Taylor," he said. "I've finished the letter this very moment."

"What about?" asked Hudson.

"Why, I wrote to ask if you were still prepared to go to China for us. We need you as soon as you can go."

3

SIX MONTHS AT SEA

SLOWLY the little sailing-ship moved away
from the wharf, carrying just sufficient sail to
bear her out into the river. Beyond the docks,
Hudson could see the narrow streets of old Liverpool, the houses huddling together up the hill-
side towards the windmill and the green fields in
the distance. In the September sunshine the busy
town looked friendly and homelike. But it was
not the town, or the noisy workmen on the
wharves, which held Hudson Taylor's eyes at that
moment. It was the group of three people who
had come to say good-bye to him; his mother, in
her black dress, with his father and his sister.
Suddenly he heard her cry out, though he could
not tell what she said, and saw her rush towards
the dock. She pulled up sharply at its very edge
and he saw her put her face in her hands.

There was nothing he could do or say to comfort her, for the watery gap between them was
growing wider. All he could do was to wave, and
go on waving until the figures in the distance were
so small that he could not distinguish them any

longer. He had never thought he could feel so miserable or lonely in his life. Every mile the ship travelled would take him further away from everything he knew and loved, and, with only sailing-ships to link East and West, letters would take months to go and come. In a day when there were no aeroplanes, no telephones and very few railways, China seemed a very long way indeed from Yorkshire.

*   *   *

The *Dumfries*, a small, 650-ton vessel with Hudson as its only passenger, came close to disaster almost before the voyage had properly begun. As they rounded the Welsh coast and drew out into the Irish Channel the sunshine was blotted out by dark clouds which rolled up over the horizon until the whole sky was filled with the menace of a storm. The swell gave place to huge waves which crashed against the side of the ship and swept across its decks. Sailors scurried to and fro battening down the hatches. Above them, the sails crashed like thunder in the heavy wind and the ropes creaked with the strain. Instead of easing as the hours went by, the fury of the storm increased. The dull light changed to darkness as the evening wore on, but it was a darkness illuminated by almost continual flashes and forks of lightning. The waves were tremendous; they towered over the ship at one moment and, the next, lifted it high into the air so that, as it crashed into the trough beyond, Hudson felt sure that it must break in pieces. There was no comfort to be had from the captain, for his bearded face was grim with anxiety.

"Never known a worse storm, in any part of the world," was the only answer Hudson received to his frightened questions. Desperately he thought of his mother, of China, and tried to pray, but no words would come to his mind. He fumbled his way downstairs and flung himself on his bunk and tried to sleep. The wooden walls of the ship shuddered as each wave broke against the side, and every part of the cabin, and indeed of the whole ship, seemed to creak and groan.

It was almost midnight when Hudson staggered up on deck once more. Now, near at hand, he caught sight of a flashing light.

"Holyhead lighthouse," shouted the captain. "We'll never clear the rocks!"

"The lifeboats?"

"They'd never live for five minutes in this sea. And if we crowd on more sail, the masts are almost certain to snap. Then, we're finished completely!" Nevertheless, he roared an order to the sailor by his side. In danger of being flung from the rigging every minute, the man began to climb up the mast. Now, however, Hudson's mind was calmer, though shipwreck seemed certain. "Let not your heart be troubled." The words came back to him as clearly as though someone had spoken them beside him.

Suddenly the captain's face cleared a little. In the darkness Hudson saw the Holyhead lighthouse seeming to move slowly behind them as the bow of the ship turned slightly towards the open sea. "The wind's changing, boy! Only a couple of points, but that's enough." He gripped Hudson's shoulder for a moment. "It's just enough, thank God. We'll clear the point and the rocks, after all!"

*   *   *

That storm was the only real excitement, apart from another occasion when they nearly drifted on to a reef in the China seas, during the whole long voyage. With no Suez Canal to shorten the journey they sailed slowly past Spain and Portugal, down the coast of Africa where the skies were grey-blue and the tropical heat drew every ounce of strength from them, round the Cape of Good Hope, across the Indian Ocean and up through the islands of South-East Asia towards the China coast. It was almost six months after leaving Liverpool, on March 1, 1854, that the captain called Hudson to the bridge and pointed ahead through the morning mist.

"Thank God for a safe arrival, my boy. There's the coast of China. See that wide river? The Yang-tze-kiang—that's its name."

"So that town . . ?"

"Aye, aye, boy. This is the end of the journey. That's Shanghai." He glanced down amongst the strange-looking boats, with their single sails, manned by thin Chinese men in homespun faded blue shirts and trousers. A trim little boat was making its way between the junks. "And here's the pilot to take us into port."

The captain was a good Christian man, who had joined Hudson in prayers each night and morning. The pilot was not, and he looked at the young missionary as if he were slightly mad. Certainly the news he brought was disturbing. "If you've got any sense, Mr. Taylor, you'll stay on this ship and go home again. The Chinese hate all foreigners, and preaching a foreign religion is asking for trouble. Asking for murder, if you want the truth."

Hudson had heard this sort of thing in England from those who criticised his missionary enthusiasm, and he was about to tell the pilot that God had sent him to China and nothing would turn him back when the captain cut in.

"Just what *is* happening in Shanghai?" he asked. "We've heard rumours about a rebellion, of course. But there are always wars going on in China."

"Oh, that's no rumour. The whole place is in an uproar. There's a rebellion against the Emperor and the rebels have occupied Shanghai. Fighting is going on all the time in the Chinese part of the town. Foreigners are more or less safe as long as they keep to their own part of the city, but I wouldn't give much for their chances outside it. Dozens of them are getting out while they're safe. Fifty thousand Imperial troops are camped outside the city and the whole place could go up in flames overnight."

"What about food?"

"Scarce. And expensive. Cost of living going up every week. Six months ago you could get five Chinese dollars for a pound; now you're lucky if you can get three. You need a lot of money to stay alive in Shanghai now, even if you escape a bullet or a knife in your back." He glared at Hudson. "Don't you think you'd better take your Bible home again?" he asked scornfully.

"I have come to stay," answered the young missionary.

"How old are you?"

"Twenty-one."

"Not old enough to be out of your mother's sight, never mind wandering round China. Where are you going when you land?"

Hudson paused, expecting another short-tempered comment at his reply. "I don't know. I have three letters from friends in England, introducing me to missionaries in Shanghai. I expect they'll help me to find somewhere to stay."

The pilot did not even answer. He merely stepped up to the ship's bridge with the captain and began to steer the ship carefully towards the distant port.

*   *   *

Once ashore, Hudson was overwhelmed with excitement. Following the guide which the captain had found for him through the crowded streets he felt as if he were dreaming. The pictures in the book he had read at Barnsley seemed to have sprung to life. The narrow alleyways, the small open shops, the coolies carrying baskets slung on long poles carried over their shoulders, the men with their pigtails and the women with their tiny feet, the thrusting crowds all talking shrilly at the tops of their voices, the faded banners with their strange writings outside the tea-houses, the heat, the noise, the smell—everything was as he had imagined it for so long, and yet far more thrilling than he had thought possible.

The excitement died away when he reached the Consulate and presented himself to the British officer whose task it was to keep in touch with all the British people in Shanghai. The officer took the three letters. He laid the first one down on the table. "This man died six months ago," he said. "And this chap"—he put the second letter on top of the first—"went back to America a week or two ago." He looked at the third letter. "Dr. Medhurst, eh? Another missionary! We've got enough of them here without you, Mr. Taylor. But we'll do our best to keep you safe as long as you don't do anything stupid like trying to go into the native quarter or up-country." He stared at the young man before him sharply. "With your white face and your fair hair you'd be in trouble straight away." He summoned a Chinese servant, who bowed gracefully as he stood inside the door, and ordered him to show Hudson the way to Dr. Medhurst's house.

Once more the young Yorkshireman made his way through the jostling crowds. Once more, too, disappointment met him at the end of the journey. At the door of the house, standing in a broad compound, another Chinese bowed, his face expressionless. He spread his hands in a gesture of regret.

"So sorry, sir. Dr. Medhurst not here. Dr. Medhurst gone away. Too dangerous to stay here any longer."

4

SHANGHAI, CHINA

HUDSON had grown accustomed to the noise of Shanghai. The hubbub of voices in the bazaars, the cries of the wandering street-sellers with their baskets on their shoulders, the temple bells, were a familiar background after a week or two. Even the more distant sound of gun-fire, rattling musket-shots and booming cannons, did not disturb him very much. Now, however, the sounds outside his new home were more shrill and piercing, and he stepped to the door to see what was going on. Only a little way off was a narrow waterway, separating the Chinese city from the International Settlement, the part of Shanghai where foreigners lived—almost a city in itself, with bigger houses, wider squares and better buildings than the congested alleyways of the old city. The noise he had heard was from a party of soldiers, encouraged or jeered at by the bystanders, removing the bridge made of a few sturdy planks which crossed the river. It was done as he watched, and the soldiers settled themselves down to guard the spot where the bridge had stood.

He felt suddenly cold, as the bright colours of the sunset faded in the sky. Followed by the hostile glances of the crowd he stepped into his Chinese house and closed the flimsy door. He felt utterly alone in the old city. Each night, he knew, would be the same. The bridge that spanned the river would be removed every night and replaced in the morning. Soldiers would be responsible for the safety of those across the river during the hours of darkness, and the crossing points would be carefully guarded against the rebels. But Hudson was alone. He had chosen to live in danger and he could blame nobody but himself if he were killed. He had already seen men and women murdered by the rebels in the narrow streets and, further up the twisting road, only a few yards away, cannonballs had demolished a couple of houses the day he moved in. It was all very well to say that he trusted God to look after him, but there were plenty of people who would say that he ought to look after himself more carefully as well. The trouble was that nothing else but this dangerous place was left to him.

*　　　*　　　*

On the day of his arrival, when he had discovered that the Medhursts had left for a safer place than the London Missionary Society's compound to which he had been brought, Hudson had felt completely lost. The servant, not knowing that he was a new arrival but assuming he was merely another Shanghai European, had gone indoors, leaving Hudson to walk disconsolately across the compound. As he did so an English voice hailed him and he turned to see a missionary coming from a house a little further away.

"My name is Edkins," said the young man. "Can I help you?"

Hudson had never been more thankful to see another Englishman in his life. Edkins took him home, introduced him to Dr. Lockhart and Mr. Wylie and sent down to the ship for his baggage, assuring him that he was welcome to stay with them as long as he cared. They raised their eyebrows a little when they heard that he had been sent by the China Evangelisation Society.

"I hope you get money sent out to keep you going, old man," said Edkins. "That Society of yours is good at sending missionaries but not so good at paying them!" Seeing Hudson's troubled face, he went on quickly, "Anyway, you can stay here with us as a paying guest until you're fixed up with a house."

Hudson discovered that Edkins' statement was only too sadly true. The China Evangelisation Society, which had paid for his passage, had few supporters and little money, though they had not told him this when they appointed him to

Shanghai. What they did send him was far too little to pay for a house in the International Settlement. For a few months he stayed with Dr. Lockhart, helping with his medical work, learning the language more quickly than most people were able to do, and, as soon as he was able, trying to preach simple sermons and tell the stories of Jesus in the streets. The fact that he was stoned and chased away time after time did not worry him. What did make him anxious was that he could not continue to be a burden to the Lockharts for ever.

One afternoon he came back from the Chinese city with a determined air. "I expect you'll think I'm mad," he said, "but I've rented a ramshackle old house in the city." He held up his hand to stop their protests. "Refugees from the country, trying to escape from the soldiers, are willing to pay £10 for a couple of rooms here in the safer places. I've only got half that amount to live on and do my work for a month, even if the Society pays me regularly. It's no use. I'm moving out to-morrow."

*   *   *

It was just as well that Hudson had a sense of humour as well as a great faith in God. In the shadowy rooms and creaking passages of the big, tumbledown house he was able to laugh at the ghosts which were supposed to haunt them, and on more than one occasion when death seemed to be just round the corner his faith helped him to laugh at real danger in just the same way. One such time was when, with Edkins and another young missionary, he set out to preach to the boatmen at Woosung Island, three hours' sailing from the mainland.

As the little junk moved through the harbour, its single, large sail billowing in the wind, the three men looked up at the big hulls of the Imperial warships. The Emperor's fleet was anchored in the harbour to try and prevent the approach of the rebels to the town, and at night the sound of their guns roared out over the city as they fired on shipping which might have contained rebel troops stealing quietly across the water. The missionaries reached Woosung Island before midday, talked to the families which made their homes in the innumerable large and small boats there, sold or gave away tracts and gospels and, in Hudson's case, found good practice for the Chinese he was now learning to speak quite fluently. Throughout the afternoon their own boatmen grew more and more restive and, when the missionaries put off their return to the mainland until it was nearly dark, they were almost panic-stricken. Only when the junk began to edge its way past the warships did the young men realise the reason. Pink skins and fair hair were enough to guarantee their safety in the daylight, but who could tell they were foreigners and neutrals in the dark? demanded the frightened Chinese boatmen. The sound of a ship sailing across the water was enough to make the sailors train a gun on them and blow them to pieces. Hudson realised the danger clearly now.

"Pink devils! Pink devils going to Shanghai!" shouted the boatmen, in shrill voices.

There were no answering hails and the missionaries imagined the guns turning in their direction. Suddenly Hudson had an idea, and across the quiet water his voice all at once rang out. "The spacious firmament on high!" Immediately Edkins and his companion joined in the hymn. As they slowly passed under the warships they went on singing at the tops of their voices, hymn after hymn, until they were hoarse with an hour's singing. The boatmen stared at the "mad foreigners" but the sailors in the ships ceased to aim their guns. Such singers could only be "pink devils" as the boatmen had said. The danger was past. As the lights of the city drew nearer the three men joined in prayer and then, led by Hudson, burst into laughter.

*   *   *

It was not always so easy to see the funny side of

things, however, in the old city. In the six months Hudson remained there the rebels drew nearer. Fires were a nightly occurrence as cannon-balls overturned lights and set fire to the flimsy walls. Musket-shots spattered against his own home. Soon, the rebels had pressed so far through the city that their guns stood at the end of the street where he lived, pointing threateningly along the crowded thoroughfare.

The end came one night when he wakened to the sound of musket-fire. There was an acrid smell and smoke curled into the room. He reached above his head and grasped the lifebelt which he always kept there, in case he had to run for his life and swim across the river to safety. Quickly he climbed the stairs and emerged on the roof. Shots whistled past him and he dodged down again, but he had time to see that the house next door was already on fire. A cannon-ball crashed into the lower part of his own home and, down below, he could hear fighting going on in the street. Showers of sparks blew from the burning house on to his own roof, and he tried to put them out, but had to leave the roof because of the gun-fire. To run into the street and try to swim across the river would be like suicide; to stay where he was might mean that he would be burned to death. Either was a grim alternative but, as he had felt a year earlier when the *Dumfries* was almost shipwrecked, so he felt again now. He could trust God to care for him, for he did not believe that God had called him to work in China only to let him die when his work had hardly begun. He prayed quietly, picked up his lifebelt and lay down on his hard bed once more. Then, above the guns, he heard a new noise, a steady, drumming sound outside, in the street and on the roof. The clouds which had been gathering throughout the day had burst in a tempest.

Hudson climbed swiftly to the roof. Standing on it, he was almost wet through in a minute or so, but he did not need to stay longer to see that the fire next door was dying down, put out by the rain which had quenched the red sparks on his own house. He thanked God silently and, with guns and thunder competing against each other outside, lay down once more and slept peacefully till dawn.

5

GO FORWARD

"I AM alone in the interior of China." When Hudson wrote those words he was only twenty-five years old, but he had faced danger and death so often that he had forgotten how to be afraid.

From the little cottage at Drainside and the bedroom he shared with his cousin in Soho while he worked at the hospital the task of preaching the gospel in China had not seemed too difficult. He had been critical of the missionary societies for not doing more work there. In the two years or so since his arrival he had seen matters more clearly. The Chinese hated all foreigners and would drive them out of China if they could; and they hated Christianity because it was a foreign religion. Many of them were bitterly opposed to anyone who preached it, and nearly everyone else seemed indifferent. Missionaries were only allowed by the British Government to live in or very near the ports, and many British officials regarded missionaries as a nuisance because they increased the Chinese dislike of foreigners. As Hudson looked at the wide mouth of the Yangtze River, emptying out the water that had travelled hundreds of miles through China, he thought of all the territory it passed through, the thousands of villages, the millions of Chinese who had never heard of Christ. *They* were the people he had come to help, and yet he could not reach them.

But, if Hudson saw the difficulties more clearly, he was also more certain than ever that God meant what He said, and that the promises which God made in the Bible were true. He found himself saying some things over and over again, to himself and to his friends.

"Never worry about money. God will always give you what is needed for His work if you trust Him."

"If it is impossible to stay where you are, go forward."

"God never promised that a missionary should be safe or free from trouble—but He *has* promised us courage and peace of mind."

*   *   *

After he had begun to learn the language, Hudson started travelling up the great Yangtze River. In his first two years he made eight river journeys, one of them two hundred miles up the banks of the Yangtze, preaching in nearly a hundred villages where no Christian had ever been seen. He made no converts, though he found people interested enough to ask him to come and preach again, but he was able to distribute scores of copies of the gospels. On the very day that he left England the Bible Society had agreed to print more copies of the Bible in the Chinese languages, and Hudson saw this as another proof that he had been right to come to China; for, now that he had started touring up the river, the Bible Society gave him all the books he needed for distribution and even paid part of his expenses—which was a very good thing since his own missionary society sent him far less than he needed to live on.

Far up-country was the town of Tungchow, and here, one day, Hudson arrived. From a distance he could see its big stone-and-mud walls firmly built to keep out invaders. The road leading to the city gate was crowded with carts, country folk going to market, soldiers and, occasionally, a sedan chair holding an important official carried by four servants. The red-brown dust covered Hudson's face and beard and got into his eyes as the crowds surged past him, turning to stare and chatter volubly, for his western coat and trousers marked him clearly enough as a despised European.

He had once imagined that all Chinese were small men, but he had quickly realised his mistake. He smiled grimly at his error once more as he approached the gate. Standing beside it was a drunken soldier, guarding the entrance to the city, and he was so tall that Hudson felt dwarfed beside him. Suddenly the soldier's hand shot out and he grasped Hudson's black coat by the collar, shouting as he did so.

"I've caught a pink devil!" he roared.

At once there was a crowd round them, collecting from the gateway, the road and the city street. Hudson was thrust one way and another, swaying about as the soldier almost lifted him off his feet. Excited voices screamed abuse and he felt his clothes being torn as bystanders snatched at him, trying to scratch his face.

"What shall we do with him?"

"Kill him!"

"Put his eyes out!"

The growing crowd shrilled their answers and jeered. Hudson knew he was nearer death than he had been when the rebels were firing down the street in Shanghai. It was useless to argue, for he could not make himself heard. Then, from the top of the wall, a soldier cried an order.

"Take him to the mandarin!"

The crowd yelled back. "No! Not the mandarin! We can deal with him ourselves! Kill the foreign devil!" But the drunken giant was now not so sure. To kill him would be pleasant enough but when the mandarin, the chief man of the town, found out there might be trouble for everyone. It would be better to let the mandarin condemn him to death, and then everything would be in order. He swung his arm round to clear the crowd and began to drag Hudson through the gate towards the *yamen*, the mandarin's headquarters. By the time they reached it the missionary's clothes were almost torn to pieces, his face was bleeding and his body black with bruises. Hudson was flung on the floor before the elderly magistrate. He stared at the calm face, the cold eyes, the wonderful silk robe, but the mandarin was not even looking at him. He was already lashing the crowd and its leaders in furious anger.

"Fools! You cannot treat Englishmen like this! I have been *taotai* of Shanghai where the foreigners live—you must treat them with respect." He went on, pointing at one man after another in the crowd as the rioters tried to shuffle out of sight. Then, at last, he turned to Hudson.

"Get up, sir! Nothing will happen to you— you are under my protection. You may preach, and distribute your books in peace."

*   *   *

The months went by. From Tungchow Hudson passed to other cities and back to Shanghai. Sometimes there was opposition, sometimes a welcome, but always there were those who bought gospels or accepted them free, promising to read them or pass them on to others. For a while he lived in the Chinese town of Tsungming, but the British consul sent for him and told him sharply that though he might travel where he liked he was not allowed to live permanently more than forty miles from one of the foreign-controlled "treaty ports". If he tried to do so without permission he would be expelled from the country by the British Government. Hudson saw little point in arguing and set off on another journey, this time with a much older and better-known missionary, William Burns.

When the two men reached Swatow, in South China, it was a new country to Hudson Taylor. They had travelled together for three months in central China and then, urged by a Christian captain on the river, had accepted a free passage in his boat to the southern capital. But there was something new about Hudson, too. Though he had blue eyes and his skin was still fair he looked less obviously a foreigner. He had decided, to the horror of his missionary friends and the scorn of other Europeans, to adopt Chinese dress and, in that way, come a little nearer to the people. He never again broke this custom on his journeys.

It would have taken more than Chinese clothing to make the missionaries welcome in Swatow.

Hudson described it as the wickedest city he had ever set foot in. No Christians lived there. It was the centre of the opium trade, and men captured by armed bands of raiders in the countryside were openly sold as coolies and slaves in the streets and markets. No one would rent the foreigners a house and they were fortunate, at last, to find lodgings in a tiny room under the roof of an incense-shop. To reach it they had to climb a rickety ladder and clamber through a trap door and, once there, they were surrounded by beetles, insects, mice, and almost suffocated by the rising smell of incense. Once more Hudson found himself the centre of sneering crowds. No one would listen to what they had to say until, at last, Hudson broke down the dislike and enmity by his skill as a doctor, as he had so frequently done before. He could never be sufficiently thankful for what he had learned with Dr. Hardey in Hull and at the London Hospital. This time it was his healing of a Chinese official who had nearly died as a result of "treatment" by local doctors that gave him his wonderful opportunity.

"He says he will give me permission to establish a sort of hospital—a very small one, of course. And there will be no opposition to our preaching in the city," he told Burns.

"But you've not enough drugs here to do that."

"No," agreed Hudson. "But I'm going back to Shanghai to get them. A month or two will see me back again and a Christian mission established in this evil place."

6

MONEY WANTED!

HUDSON saw the little group of British people watching him and chuckled to himself. The ladies were dressed as fashionably as they would have been in London, despite the fact that they had all been in Shanghai for years, and as he passed them he was very conscious of the faded, loose blue jacket and trousers and the little cap which he himself wore. They stared at him much as they would have done at a freak in a circus-show, with a look of disgust on their faces.

"It's the mad missionary, my dear," he heard one lady say to the elegant man in uniform by her side.

"Really, it shouldn't be allowed. He lets the British down wherever he goes!"

"Wanders about in the interior, so they say, preaching to the Chinese. Just as though they're ever likely to be Christians."

The officer broke in angrily. "Yes—and then one day he'll get himself captured by bandits, or murdered, or something. And we shall be told we should have prevented him making a fool of himself. Ridiculous!" He snorted. "The man should be locked up!"

It would have been no use explaining to these critical onlookers that Hudson felt himself closer to the Chinese people by dressing in their own way and talking their own language, for they had no wish to do anything of the kind. What Hudson found more trying was that many of his missionary friends could not understand, either. They, too, felt he was "showing off" by doing something different from anyone else. They would hardly have thought it possible that in a little while many missionaries to China would be following Hudson Taylor's example.

*　　*　　*

As Hudson returned from Swatow to Shanghai, however, the missionaries were in no mood to be critical. They shared his enthusiasm that it might be possible to get away from the coast and begin work in the interior of China. "It's what we'd all like to do," they said. "You know that. But our own missionary societies are a bit frightened of pioneering like that. They still want to play safe, especially in these days when there's so much anti-foreign feeling. It's only a chap like yourself, who's more or less on his own, who can do it." But they had bad news, too. It was not going to be easy to get back to Swatow and begin medical work straight away. There had been a fire in Shanghai.

"There are always fires," replied Hudson. "When I left here with William Burns we looked back once and it seemed as if there were fires all over the town. It's these Chinese bamboo houses —one overturned lamp can set them alight before you can cross the room and put the lamp out." His face grew serious. "What was lost this time?"

"I'm afraid it was your supply of drugs and medicine. We couldn't do anything to save them, Hudson. The whole lot was lost."

It was a bad blow, for Hudson had hoped to collect them and set off for Swatow at once. But worse was to come. The only thing to do was to go to Ningpo, where his friend Dr. Parker was running a hospital, and try to replace them. Drugs cost a good deal of money and Hudson, as usual, was very short of it. His own China Evangelisation Society sent less and less and he could never be sure when it would arrive. Living as cheaply as possible when he was on tour, however, he saved all he could and fortunately there would be enough to buy the drugs he needed. With a servant he set off for the distant town.

It was this servant who caused Hudson his second tragic disappointment. One night, while the missionary was asleep, the man collected £40 worth of Hudson's luggage—all he had with him and most of what he possessed—and disappeared. When he wakened, Hudson was stranded, penniless, mid-way between Shanghai and Ningpo.

With no money to waste on lodgings he camped the next night on the steps of a Chinese temple and wakened to feel a rough hand stealing under his shirt. He sat up with a jerk, caught a glimpse of a pock-marked face close to his own and tried to grab the man's wrist. Behind the first man stood two other beggar-thieves. Perhaps it was the sight of Hudson's fair hair or the sound of his Yorkshire voice that stopped them in their tracks, for, though they were three to one, they made off round the side of the temple, leaving their victim to sit up for the rest of the night in case they came back.

*   *   *

In Shanghai, after a friendly river-boat had given him a free lift back, he argued with his friends who tried to persuade him to set the police on the thieving servant. They were sure he was wrong to forgive him, to "allow him to get away with it", as they put it. And they made another point. "What are you going to do for money if you don't try and get the stuff back?" they asked.

Hudson remembered the dying woman to whom he had given his last half-crown in the Drainside slums. "I shan't worry about *that*," he replied. "God can always provide money to carry on His work—I've proved it already a good many times." He had no answer when they pointed out that he had none left. The next day, however, he had all the proof he needed that God knew when those who trusted Him were in need. He came into his missionary colleagues' home with a letter in his hand.

"Didn't I tell you?" he asked them. "God knew I was going to want help just at this moment. He answered my prayers in this morning's post from England. Here's a cheque for £40, the very amount I lost, from a Mr. Berger who's heard about the work I'm doing."

Even then, a new distress was to overwhelm Hudson. Hearing that he was about to go back to Swatow, the British consul sent for him. War had broken out between England and China and the consul forbade him to return. "Swatow," he informed him, "is in an ugly mood. There have been riots in the area against the British."

"And my friend Burns?"

"William Burns," answered the consul, "was taken prisoner and sent away to Canton—a thirty-day journey. I believe he is still safe."

Hudson had to learn to accept the misfortunes

which happened to his friends in the same way that he faced his own dangers. Unable to return to the interior, he worked for a short time in Shanghai and then in Ningpo, preaching and helping Dr. Parker in his medical work. It was here that he met a young school-teacher in the first mission school to be opened for girls in China and, from the first time they saw each other, Hudson and Maria Dyer fell in love. Soon, he began to feel that perhaps this was one of the reasons God had not allowed him to return to Swatow, for he felt that with Maria as his wife he would be able to do far more and better work as a missionary. It was not long before they were engaged to be married.

Once more, however, there was money-trouble. Hudson was responsible for feeding the patients in a little hospital which he had organized. He was due to be married, but had not enough money for a wedding and not even enough to buy rice for the hospital patients for more than a day or so. Such ready money as he possessed, some £37, he had lent to a friend who had none left and, making matters worse, he had to burn every bit of clothing he wore when a patient whom he had been nursing died of smallpox. He almost laughed at the absurdity of it all when he had a note from Maria saying she was coming to tea the following day with a friend.

"What on earth are we going to do?" asked his colleague, Mr. Jones.

"Trust God, and do the best we can to help ourselves," replied Hudson, with a faith that had been tested many times before. "But it really is ridiculous, isn't it? I'm going to entertain my fiancée, and we've no money to buy anything to eat and no clothes to wear!"

The second part of the trouble was solved almost at once. That same morning a trunk arrived with Hudson's name painted on it. His shout brought Jones running into the room. "What on earth have you got there?" he demanded.

"The answer to half our prayers." He flung the lid open. "A box of clothes which was sent on to me from Shanghai months ago. I'd given up hope of ever seeing it again." He clapped his friend gleefully on the back. "Now let's see what we can do to answer the other half. We *must* try and get some money ourselves. Let's sell something. What can we do without?" His voice was full of excitement. "There's the old stove in the kitchen."

"Yes—there's that clock, too. We could do without that. Time means nothing to these Chinese people!"

But, though a friendly merchant agreed to buy the clock, he wanted to keep it for a week to make sure it was working properly before he paid over the money. And when they carried the stove down to the river to take it to a foundry on the other side they found the shaky bridge of boats had been washed away in the night. Once more, the very day Maria was due to arrive for tea, the post brought the answer to their needs. And, again, it was Mr. Berger, who was to be so staunch a supporter of Hudson's work in the coming years, who had sent a cheque which was enough to provide food for the hospital, tea for Maria and her friend, and leave sufficient for the simple wedding.

*   *   *

Before they were married, Hudson asked Maria a rather frightening question. "You know that I believe God always answers our prayers?" Maria nodded. "And you know that I don't like the way the China Evangelisation Society who sent me here run their work? They just can't be relied on, and they're critical of many of the things I've done." Maria nodded again. "Then would you agree to break our connection with the Society altogether—to work on our own, go where we believe God sends us and trust Him to provide all we need to carry out His orders?"

It was the biggest decision either of them had ever had to make, but Maria had no doubts about the answer. Hudson wrote to London resigning from the Society. From that moment, the young married missionaries were on their own, without any promise of help from England and with only God to turn to for support.

The three years that followed were a testing-time for their faith. They began a little church in Ningpo and quickly had converts from the old Chinese religions—Tsiu, the teacher, Fang the basket maker, Wang the painter, Nyi the cotton merchant and a dozen more. This was encouraging, but the times were dangerous. Sixty Portuguese were massacred in broad daylight in an anti-foreign riot not far from the place where they lived, and in Hong Kong one of the city's bakers tried to kill all the Europeans by putting poison in their bread. More worrying still, Maria Taylor nearly died when her first baby was born. And, at last, after six years in China Hudson's own health broke down and the doctors insisted that he should return to England.

"You'll die if you stay any longer," they said, and then added another warning. "And you'll die if you come back!"

7

BRIGHTON BEACH

HUDSON and Maria, fresh from the squalor and poverty of China, gazed at the wide tree-lined roads of Bayswater, with trimly-dressed maids flitting behind the windows, and horses and carriages standing before the gracious porches with their pillars and steps. "This is no place for people like us," said Hudson. "We haven't the right kind of money or the right sort of manners!"

Maria laughed with him and then became serious. "Your sister Amelia and her husband have asked us to stay here till you're better. You'll have to learn your manners all over again, even if it does mean practising how to use a knife and fork instead of chop-sticks!"

"It's very good of them, certainly. But I'd be happier in a tiny house of my own."

"We'll get one as soon as you're fit again, Hudson. But don't forget that if your dreams for China are going to come true you're going to need all the help people like this can give you."

Hudson nodded, knowing his wife was right.

The doctors had sent him home from China, almost in a state of collapse after years of hard work, and the English doctors had told him the same thing as his friends in China. "You ought never to go back—certainly not to the same kind of life as you've been leading. Settle into a big town; have some comfort; look after yourself. But none of this pioneering business in remote villages with too little food and nobody to care whether you live or die." Now, friends who had heard of his work and read the many articles he wrote for Christian magazines in Britain, had offered help to Hudson and his wife for the time being. Well-fed, sleeping properly, surrounded by friends who were interested in his work, he began to recover.

"I'll soon be able to go back to China after all," he said one day to Maria. "But first of all I'm going to qualify properly as a doctor. We'd better get a small house near the London Hospital. I'll go back there, where I started, and get my medical diplomas."

"The doctors were very definite, you know," said his brother-in-law, Mr. Broomhall. "They said you ought not to go."

Hudson smiled over the ignorance of doctors. He was one himself, so he knew all about them, he thought. "God was definite, too—and He told me I *must* go!" He walked urgently up and down the room, and they saw that he had put on a good deal of weight and the strained look was gone from his face. "Of course, I don't belong to a missionary society any longer. I haven't anyone to support me, or to support any worker I take with me. But God has never let us down so far—even though we've often been reduced to our last ounce of rice or our last small copper *cash*. We must just rely on Him."

Mr. Broomhall looked at his wife and then back at Hudson. "You can rely on us, too. I think God wants us to help you if you go back or if you send anyone else. And we have a good many friends who are anxious to do the same."

*   *   *

Hudson began to feel certain that some of his dreams were beginning to come true. But they were very big dreams indeed—so big that some who read his articles could only smile at their wildness, while others determined they must do all they could to support him. He and Maria moved into a small house in Whitechapel, near the London Hospital, and Hudson divided his working time between studying there, writing books and articles, and preaching.

One afternoon a young man named Meadows knocked at the door and stared in surprise when it was opened by a thin Chinese man in blue shirt and trousers, Wang the painter, with a slender black pigtail down his back.

"Come with me," he said, as he trotted down the passage. "Master is in his room." The door was thrown open and Meadows found himself facing a slim, bearded man of thirty who rose from a table covered with books and papers. It was not Hudson Taylor who held his attention for the moment, however, but the huge map of China spread out on the wall. "I've come to the right place," he commented. "Your servant and the map on the wall show that clearly enough. My name is Meadows," he went on, "and I've come to see if you can send me to China."

Hudson remembered how he had once visited the Congregational minister in Barnsley, and how his friend had put all sorts of difficulties in his way. Now, to his astonishment, he found himself beginning in much the same way. "I believe God wants me to go back to China myself some day. And I'm sure He needs workers there and wants me to send them. But I don't belong to any society. And I'm not a missionary society myself, either," he smiled. "I'll do all I can to support you, but I can't promise you any exact salary. You'll have to go in faith, believing that if you're really called to the task God will support you—though sometimes right up to the last minute you'll wonder if He's heard your prayers or noticed your need. I can only use people who trust God absolutely and utterly, as I do myself."

Words like those were to be spoken in the years that followed to everyone who wanted to join Hudson Taylor's great work in China. From the beginning it was a "faith mission". Meadows was clear that this was exactly what he wanted to do—and his wife, too. Hudson took him over to the map.

"When God said 'Go for Me to China' I don't think He meant 'go where it is safe . . . go where there are Europeans . . . go to the treaty ports and the coast.' I think He meant 'Go on . . . go inland . . . go everywhere!' " He pointed to the big map. "Mr. Meadows, there are two hundred million people in the interior of China who have never heard of Jesus Christ! Eleven whole provinces without a single missionary! Those are the people and places I want to reach—with the help of men like you."

"I'm sure there will be many like me who will want to go."

Hudson hardly seemed to have heard. He was stabbing his finger here and there on the map. "Eleven provinces. Listen to their names—West of the River, Four Streams, Clear Sea, North of the Lake, South of the Clouds. With God's help we will win them all for Him!"

*   *   *

It was not as easy as Hudson's enthusiasm made it sound. Though Meadows and his wife— Hudson's first workers—went to China the following year it was three years before the next three volunteers joined them. Hudson worked at the London Hospital, preached, lectured and wrote, wearing himself out almost as much as he had done in China, but after five and a half years back in England his dream of the eleven inland provinces all occupied by courageous missionaries seemed hardly nearer fulfilment than when he returned home. What was wrong? he kept asking himself and his friends. Had he not told enough people, not put the situation clearly—or were the people of Christian Britain not worried about missionary work, after all?

One day the answer seemed to leap to his mind quite clearly. When he needed money and had asked God for it, God had always answered his prayers. When he asked for someone to go to China, God had sent Meadows and three other men. There could be only one reason why God had not sent still more helpers—Hudson himself had not made his prayers big enough. "I have not been given more because I have not asked for more," he told Maria.

It was just at this time that a great friend,

George Pearse, asked him to spend a few days on holiday at Brighton. On the Sunday he felt he simply could not go to church. There would be a thousand people in the congregation, all thanking God for their own good things and none of them concerned about China, India, Africa or anywhere else but Brighton—or so it seemed to Hudson. Instead of turning in at the church he walked on until he came to the sands and there, to and fro, he paced up and down, hardly noticing the sea or the June sunshine. He talked to God as he walked. "I've been thinking of this as *my* mission, *my* work in China," he said, "but it isn't. It's *your* mission. *You* must send the men and women. But," he went on quite practically, "I know how many we need to begin with." Taking his Bible from his pocket he began to write.

Prayed for twenty-four willing, skilful labourers at Brighton, June 25, 1865.

There *must* be twenty-four, he thought—two for each of the eleven provinces, and two for Mongolia, which he had not counted before.

He walked back across the sand and the pebbles, watched by gentlemen in tight trousers and top-hats, and ladies in fashionable, full-skirted silk dresses. He did not notice them, any more than he realised that his feet were soaking wet. His face was happier than it had been for many months. He not only felt, he *knew*, that something quite new had begun. Back at Mr. Pearse's house he told his host that he must go back to London the next day. He had something very important to do. He arrived in London too late but on the Tuesday morning he set off for the bank and asked to see the manager.

"I want to open a new account," he told the dignified, whiskered gentleman behind the large desk.

"Yes." The manager nodded. The serious young man did not seem as though he had much money. "How much are you going to pay in?"

Hudson sounded as excited as if he were paying in ten thousand pounds. "Ten pounds."

"*Ten* pounds!" The manager rubbed his nose. "I see. And your name, sir?"

"Oh, it isn't for me," answered Hudson hurriedly. "It is a new missionary society. It began two days ago. The money is all I have towards it so far."

"And what is its name?"

"The China Inland Mission," replied Hudson, laying the money on the manager's desk.

8

CHINA INLAND MISSION

"WHEN are you hoping to sail?"

"In May."

"*May?*" Colonel Puget looked at the man who had come to spend the night with him at his Hertfordshire home. "But it's May now!"

"Yes," replied Hudson, "but it's only the *first* of May."

"And no arrangements made about which ship you're sailing on?"

Hudson did not seem at all worried as he answered. "Not yet, Colonel. I've sent out a lot of inquiries, of course, to different shipping companies. But I don't know whether we have enough money in the C.I.M. account to pay what they ask."

"C.I.M.?"

"China Inland Mission," Hudson explained. "You'll get used to the initials soon. I hope people will be using them long after they've forgotten J.H.T. James Hudson Taylor," he added hurriedly, seeing the puzzled look on the

Colonel's face. "*I'm* not very important, except that God has used me to begin the Mission."

He *had* begun the Mission. By obeying God's voice he had run into all sorts of dangers and opened himself to bitter criticism, but he was quite certain that God would keep all His promises. "Every difficulty can be overcome by faith," he used to say to those who thought he was too adventurous or foolish in his plans. But he was careful to try and be sure that his plans were God's plans, not just his own ideas—even though he seemed to act as if the more impossible a scheme looked, the more likely it was that this was just what God wanted him to do.

No one, for instance, would have decided to recruit twenty-four untried missionaries for China unless he were sure that God was behind him. To Hudson, the proof of this was that before eight months had passed there were twenty-four men and women ready to go. No one, with only £10 in the bank, would have started to book accommodation for his party unless he had Hudson's faith. "We need £2,000," he told his wife, Maria, as soon as he began to figure out the cost. "Then let us pray every day that God will send it," she had answered. The daily prayer meeting began at noon that day and went on through the weeks and months. On February 6, Hudson sent a booklet to the printer which he proposed to distribute to all his supporters and he was able to say that he had already received £1,500 of the £2,000. Because the booklet was not published until March, however, he had to insert a blue slip in it saying that he then had £1,974. The wonderful thing was that he had never asked anyone, even his closest friends, for a penny. Nor had he taken a collection at any of his meetings all over the country. He and his wife had prayed—and the wonderful answer to their prayers had come.

*   *   *

But, at the beginning of May, though he had his helpers ready to go and some £2,000 ready to pay the fare, there was still no news of a ship. And, as Hudson knew very well, it might cost even more than he already had. With Colonel Puget presiding over the meeting that night in Hertfordshire he told those who had come how things had gone so far. He spent little time over money. Instead, as he always did, he talked about China— the villages he had stayed in, the adventures he had been through, the need of millions of people who knew nothing of Jesus.

"You *must* take a collection," whispered Puget, as Hudson sat down.

"I have never done so—and I won't." The missionary's voice was authoritative.

"You're wrong, you know," muttered the chairman as he rose to thank the speaker. Hudson still shook his head.

Next morning the postman brought a letter and Hudson opened it at breakfast. As he was reading it the Colonel entered the breakfast-room. "I told you it was only the beginning of May, didn't I?" he asked. "Look! We've been offered passages for everybody on the *Lammermuir*, my wife and our four children included. Cabin class, too!"

The Colonel raised his eyebrows. "Cabins, eh? But that's very expensive, surely?"

"You're quite right. Missionaries aren't used to such luxury. And we haven't enough money. But God will send it."

Puget reached over the table, passing a little bundle of cheques across to Hudson. "He has, my dear friend." Hudson looked at the top ones. "They came from some of the people at the meeting last night. And you were quite right about the collection, Mr. Taylor. If you had taken one I would have put £5 in it. But I couldn't sleep all night for thinking of what you told us about the inland provinces of China. God changed my mind for me." He passed over another cheque signed by himself. "This should help to pay for the cabins." Hudson looked down at the cheque and found it hard to believe his eyes.

It was made out to the China Inland Mission, and was for £500.

*　　*　　*

Hudson had already sent ten young missionaries to China. Twenty-two people, including his own family, made up the *Lammermuir* party. He had the twenty-four willing workers he had asked for on Brighton beach, and it might be thought that all his troubles were over. Instead, they were only just beginning. The little sailing-ship ran into two typhoons and it was not surprising that many of the passengers feared for their lives. The first broke the main-mast, leaving the ship floundering, and the second almost wrecked it. Yet, as he soon discovered, storms at sea were nothing to the storms that broke on his arrival in Shanghai.

Instead of being welcomed by the British community and the missionaries, he found himself and his party criticised from all sides. Many of the officials were certain that missionaries going into the remote country districts would be attacked and killed. They should be forbidden to go. Even if nothing happened to them their very presence might rekindle the old hatred for foreigners and result in riots even in Shanghai. The Chinese newspapers published bitter criticisms, and lately he had heard that newspapers in

Britain were attacking him and even in the House of Commons his plan for a mission to inland China was angrily opposed and attempts made to stop it. What hurt him more than anything else was the attitude of some of the missionaries already in China, who opposed him as a dreamer and almost as a madman for wanting to penetrate deep inland, without any certainty of money being available to keep the Mission going.

Hudson gave up reading the newspapers, left his friends to fight on his behalf in Parliament, was as polite to the other missionaries as they would allow him to be, and began to plan the details of his advance into some of the eleven "unoccupied" provinces. "West of the Mountains", "South of the Clouds", "North of the Lake"—their lovely Chinese names stood for huge areas which no Christian had ever visited, and Hudson started the first of his new journeys to settle his workers in them. He soon found that the forecasts of the British in Shanghai were quite true. It seemed as if nobody would have anything to do with the new missionaries. More important, he proved again that God never left them completely stranded. Help always came, even if it was at the last minute.

In Shanghai, with not enough money to hire a house, Hudson had a message from an acquaintance who felt sorry for them—a Mr. Gamble who offered the party his *go-down*, or store-shed, for the time being. When they pressed on inland they had to move from town to town, for the sentries at the gates refused to allow them to enter, until at last they arrived at Hangchow. Here, after Hudson had looked at more than thirty houses and been turned down each time, a Mr. Kreyer lent them his house for a week while he himself was absent—and on the very last day of the week Hudson was able to rent a Chinese building for them.

It was real pioneering. Here and there, in one town after another, Hudson stationed his workers, sometimes two together, sometimes one by him-self. Riots occurred wherever they settled. Money was slow in coming, though it always arrived in time. Their living-quarters were rough-and-ready in the extreme and, sometimes, almost unbear-able to well-bred folk who had always had knives and forks, servants to wait on them and good carpets on the floor. Instead, whatever they had been used to in England, they had leaky roofs, filth-encrusted floors and an unappetising diet of boiled rice. But Hudson always seemed to get the roughest place of them all. "It's pretty cold," he wrote back to England, "to be living in a house without any ceiling . . . with very few walls and windows . . . and with a big hole, six feet by nine, in the wall of my bedroom, covered over by a sheet!"

*　　*　　*

A year went by—the hardest year Hudson had ever known, but by the end of it he felt more sure than ever that the Mission was part of God's plan for China. There were, by that time, eight stations occupied by his workers, some of the cities having several missionaries at work in them and travelling in the villages round about. The two furthest were almost a month's journey apart, so it was easy to see that the work was spreading. Six months after their arrival one of the *Lammermuir* party had died, but that only made the rest eager to work even harder.

Then, something much worse happened. Gracie, born a year after he and Maria were married, fell ill. There were no doctors near at hand, but Hudson was a doctor himself and knew better than most people how to deal with the many sicknesses of China. Neither his skill nor all the prayers of his friends and colleagues could save her from the terrible disease she had contracted. Eight years old, Gracie Taylor died, and was the first of Hudson's family to be buried in China. Two others of his children were to die there, and it was to be only three years before his wife, Maria, too, was to die at Chinkiang.

His friends watched and waited to see what Hudson would do after Gracie's death. Would he send the family home? Or go back to the coast, where he could direct the operations of the Mission more safely? They might easily have guessed the answer.

"We must go forward," announced Hudson, and his wife agreed. "We must press on to Chinkiang."

"Father," asked one of the younger children, "where is this place Chinkiang?"

Hudson smiled and unrolled his map. "Here!" He stabbed with his finger. "Chinkiang is the gateway of China!"

9

NEVER TO WALK AGAIN

THE streets of Yangchow were thronged
with people. Smells from the incense shops
mixed with the stench of the dirty drains. Faded
signs and scrolls, hanging from the shops, dangled
limply in the breathless afternoon air. Beggars
edged their way through the alleyways, making
for the temples where they would sit on the steps
collecting alms from the worshippers. Shop-
keepers shouted their wares, customers argued
about prices or quality in shrill voices, bells
jangled, porters shouted angrily to make way
for the important people they carried in the
chairs suspended on poles from their shoulders.
Everywhere there was noise and confusion. And
then, slowly, as if someone had given an order for
silence, the noise and shouting gave place to
sibilant whispering.

In the near-silence a group of newcomers made
their way through the street towards the central
market-place. The men wore Chinese clothes,
and so did their women and children, but it was
easy to see they were not Chinese. Their faces

were pink and the children's hair not dark enough.

"Foreign devils!"

"Pink devils!" The silence was broken by a shout, and then another, and another.

"Why have they come?" "Get rid of them!" "They'll bring bad luck to the city!"

From the back of the crowd which gathered round them some rotten vegetables, picked up underneath a market stall, flew through the air and landed on the leading man's chest, spattering it with filth, splashing into his face. It was quickly followed by more, and harder, missiles, as the angry shouts grew swiftly into a tumultuous roar and the frightened crowd turned into a violent mob.

*   *   *

Hudson had expected trouble, for anti-foreign riots had broken out again in China. French priests and nuns had been massacred in more than one town. He felt certain that he would be unwelcome, but he knew that God had preserved him in a good many tight corners and he hoped that the presence of the women and children would prevent real violence. Instead, the sight of British women seemed to make the people angrier than ever, and before long, he was to be involved in the worst riot he had ever known.

The mandarin of Yangchow hated all foreigners and, for many weeks, prevented Hudson finding a house to live in. Every time the British consul tried to help the missionaries the mandarin upset the arrangements. When, at last, they did manage to rent a house as a headquarters for the mission, shop-keepers were reluctant to sell them food and no one would listen to their preaching. What puzzled Hudson more than this was that the anger on people's faces seemed to give way to a new look of fear and horror. If he had heard the gossip which was going round the bazaar he would have understood more quickly.

"These foreign devils have come to steal our people and sell them for slaves."

"There are children missing already," the rumour went.

"They worship a foreign god who feeds on children!"

Still worse grew the rumours, spreading faster through the town and into the countryside. "Their god lives on little children."

"They steal our children in the darkness and eat them in their mission house."

"There are twenty-two children missing now!"

*   *   *

Hudson had hardly heard anything of all this and though he saw the temper of the people growing more ugly he still did not expect the violence that broke out one evening. The first sign of it was a noise like a storm in the distance. Hudson stood in the open doorway and listened. "A riot, I think," he commented. "In the market-square." His wife Maria joined him. "It's a big crowd, too. And they're coming this way!"

Maria looked at him. "You don't think they're making for the Mission?"

"They might be. The consul warned us to look out for trouble." He took his wife's hand in a firm grip. "Don't be afraid, Maria."

"I have never been afraid yet . . . not really afraid . . . not for ourselves, at any rate." The noise grew louder still. "If they attack us you must try and get away in the darkness and fetch help from the mandarin. Even if he hates foreigners he daren't let anything happen to us."

"I'll try. Duncan"—one of his fellow-missionaries—"had better come with me. One of us ought to get through, anyway." He thrust Maria into the house as the leaders of the mob came in sight, and stood alone under the shadow of the overhanging, curved roof. "Perhaps I can talk them into leaving us alone."

He soon saw the foolishness of that hope. With stones battering against the house he knew he would be killed if he stayed outside and, as a half-brick splintered against the wall near his head, he turned swiftly, ducked into the house and slammed the bolts into place as soon as he had closed the door. There was no chance of quietening the mob and, as it seemed, little chance of escape, though the crowd contented themselves with stone-throwing and shouting insults. Not until night fell did Hudson and Duncan ask Maria to keep the crowd's interest at the front of the house while they climbed out through a window at the back. In their Chinese dress, keeping their heads down and scarves across their faces, they slipped out of the compound, joined the milling throng, shouting as if they were themselves part of the rioters, and gradually eased their way through it until they were free to run through the deserted streets. Even then, it was half an hour before they reached the *yamen* to seek the help of the mandarin.

The cynical-looking official listened to their story, promised to investigate—and shut them up in a closed room for forty-eight hours. For those two days they heard no news from the Mission and all they could do was pray for the safety of their families and friends, not even knowing if they were still alive.

Yangchow was, for many years, to remain in Hudson's mind as a place of tragedy. Maria and the rest of the missionaries were able to escape from the house, though they were badly injured as they dropped from upstairs windows when the rioters finally set the house on fire. The temporary Mission headquarters were destroyed, and the chance of doing effective work there seemed very slight indeed. Though the mandarin set Hudson and Duncan free after two days' imprisonment, and the violence of the mob died away, the hostility of the townsfolk remained.

There were other tragedies, too. When in time they reached Chinkiang, one of his children died not long after their arrival in the city and, before two years had gone by, an epidemic of cholera swept through the town. Maria, weakened by hardship and a slim diet of rice, caught the dreadful disease and, like her last baby, only two days old, died and was buried in the little cemetery which the Mission had opened for their Christian workers. Through all these sad days Hudson never for a moment lost his faith or doubted that God would give him the strength and courage to go on working for China.

*　　　*　　　*

There did come a time, however, when he wondered about the future. This was a few years later. He had been travelling on a river boat. The stairway down to the hold, where he had found some cheap accommodation, was dirty and slippery and, as he was climbing down, his feet shot away from him and he crashed to the bottom of the steps. For a while he could not even stand and when he managed to get to his feet he clutched his back in agony. At first he thought it was broken, and he had to lie down until he could reach a doctor.

"You've been told this kind of thing before, I know, Mr. Taylor. But this time it's true, I'm afraid." The doctor looked solemn. "You must go home."

"China is more my home than anywhere else now."

"I mean back to England. You're finished, as far as China is concerned . . . as far as *any* kind of work is concerned, I'm afraid. You haven't broken your back but I think you've snapped some of the nerves or something of the kind. You won't ever be able to walk again." He saw the unbelief in Hudson's face. "Nothing will make any difference, Mr. Taylor—not even praying about it!"

For more than a year it seemed as if the doctor's verdict was only too true. Indeed, things were worse than he had suggested. Back in England Hudson lay on his bed, unable to walk or even sit up. As the weeks went by he found he could not move his arms and his hands were so paralysed that it was impossible to hold a pen or write a letter.

"Your work is finished." Hudson remembered the doctor's dreadful words. "Not even prayer will help you now."

But Hudson knew that even if prayer would not help *him*—and he was not convinced of that—it would certainly help China. He had a big map pinned to the foot of his bed so that it was always in sight. Two of the provinces for which he had planned were "occupied". Nine others, out of the eleven, had no missionaries. Day after day, and through the nights when the pain kept him awake, he prayed for China.

*   *   *

The doctor was wrong.

Hudson did walk again and, more than that, he went back to China. With him he took a group of new missionaries. Recalling how Jesus had sent out seventy disciples to preach and heal, he began to figure out on a piece of paper just how many *he* needed to fill the stations he had in mind. To his astonishment he discovered that he, too, needed seventy. There was not enough money to send them, or keep them when they were sent, but that did not worry Hudson. He wrote about his "Seventy" in his magazines and papers—and, before many months had gone by, he had over four hundred volunteers from whom to choose. By the time the Seventy were on their way to China the money coming into the China Inland Mission was well on its way to being double what it had been before.

Hudson soon found that seventy was not nearly enough. He needed a hundred . . . five hundred . . . a *thousand* new workers. And, in five years, there were not only a thousand but one thousand one hundred and fifty-three new missionaries in China. The great missionary knew the time had come to give up pioneering. Adventures in the interior of China must be left to others. He himself would have more than enough to do in organising the work, visiting the many centres of the Mission, and speaking about it in Britain, Europe and America. Nearly everyone seemed to have heard of the C.I.M. and its wonderful work in places where no missionary had been before—and throughout the world people wanted to know still more.

10

SOUTH OF THE LAKE

IN the garden of a charming little house at La Chiesaz, in Switzerland, an old man put down his binoculars. It was quite dark, though it was not yet time for bed, and he had spent the past hour looking at the stars. Binoculars were easier to hold than a telescope when a man was over seventy and had been ill for nearly four years. He shivered a little in the evening breeze, gathered his coat round him more tightly and went indoors.

An elderly lady, lying in bed, smiled at him as he went into the bedroom. "The stars again, Hudson?" she teased. "Don't you ever get tired of watching them?"

"No more than you tire of looking at the flowers I bring you every day," he answered, gently. "How do you feel to-night?"

"Not too well. I don't think I shall be with you much longer." Hudson turned away to hide the tears in his eyes. "What will you do when I'm gone, and you're all alone?"

The old man lifted his head, turned back and

stood with his hands clasped behind his back. He seemed to be seeing things very far away. "When I look at the stars, I think of how I slept under them so often in China. When I look at Lake Geneva, down there at the foot of these hills, I think of the brown hills of China. I think of Changsha, the province that we called 'South of the Lake'—our Chinese lake—and remember that it was the last of the eleven provinces we marked out so long ago. The Mission is there now, too. God has done what He promised, so many years ago, on the beach at Brighton. He has opened the way for us to preach His word in every province of inland China. When you're here no longer, and I'm quite alone . . ." His voice was steady now, but he stopped speaking in the middle of the sentence.

"Yes?"

"I think I would like to go back to China. For the last time, my dear."

Neither of them said any more. His sick wife was too tired to talk and Hudson's thoughts were far away.

*　　　*　　　*

Soon after his first wife, Maria, had died in Chinkiang and he had returned to England he had married again. He needed a wife to help him and to care for the children that were left, and for more than thirty years they had lived, worked and travelled together. It was his second wife who had helped to nurse him back to health when he was paralysed after his fall down the Chinese ship's hold. Much of the time they had had to be parted, for Mrs. Taylor was needed in England and Hudson spent as much time in China during those thirty years as he did at home. Indeed, he soon saw that for the rest of his life he could no longer be a pioneer, facing the dangers of riot and the difficulties of establishing new mission centres. He was a builder, as well as an adventurer, and his real work after those first twenty exciting years was to make the China Inland Mission the greatest of all the missionary societies working in China.

The old days of suspicion and antagonism had gone. Hudson Taylor was an honoured name amongst all missionaries. The new schemes he had brought in were being followed by other societies—women at work alone in the interior, schools for missionaries' children, striking out into the country instead of sticking safely in the coastal towns. Time after time he went back to China to see for himself what was happening, to guide and encourage the men and women on the spot; but always he had to come back home again to work in the Mission headquarters or to travel in Scandinavia, Germany, America or some other country speaking about the Mission's work and interviewing those who wished to join its thousands of workers.

This sort of work, together with endless writing and speaking, was as tiring as working in some remote corner of inland China. When he was almost seventy he collapsed in America, after a long preaching tour that had taken him from China to Australia and New Zealand and on to the United States. His wife was ill, too, and when he eventually reached England his friends decided that he must give up all his responsibilities and go and live as quietly as possible in Switzerland, where they found a house for the two invalids in the hills above Lake Geneva.

The doctors had long ago given up arguing with him. One after another had told him that he could never go back to China, and yet he had always returned, stronger and more vigorous than before. Now, however, they did not need to argue. He found it difficult enough, at first, even to walk along the road that gave such lovely views of the great Swiss lake. Certainly, too, he could not leave his wife. But, as the years passed, he seemed to grow a little stronger once more. He still wrote a great deal, and with the beautiful alpine flowers to cheer him in the daytime, for he had always loved flowers, and his binoculars to range the skies at night, some of the old vigour came back to him. His eyes cleared and his shoulders were set more firmly. Then, in the summer of 1904, Mrs. Taylor died and was buried in the little Swiss churchyard.

In the spring of 1905 Hudson Taylor sailed for China for the last time.

*   *   *

He landed in Shanghai, remembering the first time he had come there, when there was no one to welcome him and he had sought refuge with the London Missionary Society's workers while all the town was in fear of destruction. Now he was given a reception in the city such as no other missionary had ever received.

He passed on to one station after another—Yangchow, where he had nearly lost his life in the tremendous riot; Ningpo, where he had first met Maria Dyer and later married her; Hangchow, where the first pioneers, some of "the twenty-four", had found refuge in friendly Mr. Kreyer's house. Finally he came to Changsha—"South of the Lake"—the last of the eleven provinces he had planned to occupy with his missionary forces. Banners welcomed him, red for joy and emblazoned with Chinese characters embroidered in gold. It was the first of June when he arrived there, a Thursday afternoon. On the Friday morning he went to see the site of a new hospital.

On the Saturday morning he spoke to Chinese Christians gathered in the chapel. In the afternoon he went to a reception, given in his honour in the mission garden by the missionaries of the town.

He reminded them again of the three things he had always believed more firmly than anything else. "God is alive," he said. "He has spoken in the Bible. And He means what He says, and will always do what He has promised."

"I've heard him say those three things time after time," murmured one missionary.

"He's said them and written them hundreds of times," added another. "They are the things on which he has based his whole life. He could never have done what he's achieved unless he believed them."

"He looks very tired," put in another. "This triumphant procession round China would take it out of any of us."

Hudson came across to them, bowing in his old ceremonious Chinese fashion as he moved from group to group. "I'm going inside to rest," he said.

They watched him go into the house. Inside, he lay down, quiet and happy. In his mind's eye he could see the map, as he once pinned it to the wall of his tiny study in the house at White-chapel. Four Streams ... South of the Clouds ...

North of the Lake . . . Clear Sea. His dreams had come true. "Go for Me to China," God had commanded him more than fifty years earlier in the chemist's shop in Barnsley. He had gone, without a doubt or a fear in his heart. He had had a long life and travelled far. But now, he was at the end of the journey. Changsha—South of the Lake. The last of them all. As the missionaries in the garden went home Hudson Taylor, with a prayer of thankfulness, fell asleep for the last time in the country he loved.